# a big bowl of
# noodles

## acknowledgements

Firstly I would like to thank Catie Ziller for offering me the opportunity to publish another book under her watchful eye. David Loftus, the biggest bear hug for making my food look so scrumdiddlyumptious. Harriet and Jemma for creating such a relaxed, warm, friendly working environment. Jane Campsie, the style queen for zipping me around London and letting me in on all her favourite propping spots. Melissa Singer, the girl with the eye, for providing me with the perfect Asian trinkets. To Chef Ruthie Cumming, thank you for the love, care and attention you put into the preparation of the recipes. To Sarah Rock for the lovely design and my editor Michelle Pickering for being so on the ball.

Now to the people without whom I know this book would not have even seen the light of day: Rob, Daz, Paulie, Penel, Millie, Erin, Birdie, Dundee, Richie, Danny, Harriet, Ben, Inga, Tim, Brent, Dave and Dave O for helping sift through and remove what was left of my life from under "the tree". Marshall and Jamie who made sure I had an office to write in, a bed to sleep in and a hug when needed. To my awesomely talented buddy Donna Hay for always being there. To everyone at donna hay mag for their kindness and gifts. Annie and Roly for the constant supportive phone calls. Shan, Geoffrey, Peter, Suzie a rainbow full of thank yous for the kindness you have shown me. The amazingly supercalafragalistic women who help me keep me on my path, Kerry, Ros, and Maria, bless.

To Penel, for being a gold medallist friend. To my mum for her superspeedy crotcheting skills that gave another special blankie. Margaret and Richard at Bookoccino for helping me begin to rebuild my most cherished cookbook library.

To Jink my darlingly delightful fairy flatmate, for helping put the wheels back on and for your new found love of cooking. To Jed, for bringing a pramsful worth of drama and egg loveliness into my life. My amazingly all inspiring blessed girlfriend Jude, who comforts, supports and nutures me as only she knows how to do. And lastly to the angels who performed a miracle on February 5, I don't know if you eat noodles up there, but this one's for you, thanks for giving me a second chance.

## credits

Mint, 70 Wigmore Street, London W1 9DL

Recipe on front cover: warm lemon squid noodle salad (page 50)

First published in 2002 by Murdoch Books UK Ltd

ISBN 1 903992 32 X

A catalogue record for this book is available from the British library.

Text copyright © Jody Vassallo 2002
Photography copyright © Murdoch Books UK Ltd 2002

**Managing Editor** Anna Cheifetz
**Project Editor** Michelle Pickering
**Art Direction and Design** Sarah Rock
**Photographer** David Loftus
**Home Economist** Ruth Cumming

**CEO** Robert Oerton
**Publisher** Catie Ziller
**Production Manager** Lucy Byrne

Colour separation by Colourscan, Singapore
Printed by Toppan Printing Co., China

Murdoch Books UK Ltd
Ferry House
51–57 Lacy Road
London SW15 1PR
Tel: +44 (0)20 8355 1480
Fax: +44 (0)20 8355 1499
Murdoch Books UK Ltd is a subsidiary
of Murdoch Magazines Pty Ltd

UK Distribution
Macmillan Distribution Ltd
Houndsmills, Brunell Road
Basingstoke, Hampshire, RG1 6XS
United Kingdom
Tel: +44 (0) 1256 302 707
Fax: +44 (0) 1256 351 437
http://www.macmillan-mdl.co.uk

Murdoch Books®
Pier 8/9, 23 Hickson Road
Miller's Point
NSW 2000 Australia
Tel: +61 (0)2 8220 2000
Fax: +61 (0)2 8220 2558
Murdoch Books® is a trademark
of Murdoch Magazines Pty Ltd

# a big bowl of
# noodles

## Jody Vassallo

PHOTOGRAPHY BY David Loftus

MURDOCH BOOKS

# contents

6    noodle basics

8    types of noodles

16    soups & snacks

38    salads

60    stir-fries

92    glossary & index

# noodle basics

In recent years the popularity of noodles has increased dramatically in the Western world. Noodles are made by combining flour, water, salt and sometimes egg to form a soft, pliable dough. The dough is fed through steel rollers several times to form a thin sheet that is then passed through cutting rollers to be cut into long ribbons. In some Asian countries the dough is rolled out and cut by hand.

It is believed that noodles originated in the north of China in 1st century AD. The Chinese then introduced noodles to Japan, where they are now thought of as a convenient fast food. Noodles also made their way south along trade routes to Thailand, Vietnam, Malaysia, Singapore and Indonesia.

Throughout Asia noodles are a symbol of longevity. In Japan, soba noodles are the last thing eaten on New Year's Eve, and in China crispy noodles are eaten on celebratory occasions such as birthdays and New Year. Cutting noodles is believed to bring bad luck. Another custom involved with eating noodles is 'slurping'. Slurping cools the noodles as you suck them into your mouth out of the hot stock, and the sound indicates that the meal is being enjoyed.

Noodles are widely available in Western and Asian food stores. Dried noodles can be found on the shelves, while fresh noodles are stored in the refrigerator. There are no strict rules about which noodles should be used in which dishes. However, thin noodles tend to soak up flavours and so are suited to soups, while thick noodles are ideal for stir-fries. If you cannot find the type of noodle used in the recipe, feel free to substitute another and adjust the cooking instructions accordingly. As a general rule of thumb, double the quantity of noodles indicated if you are substituting fresh for dried.

One thing to remember when stir-frying noodles is not to add too many to the wok at one time or you will find yourself with a soggy mass. The biggest problem with noodles is overcooking, which causes them to break up. You should therefore always follow the instructions on the packet carefully. Also remember that, if you are adding noodles to soups and stir-fries where they will be reheated, they need not be cooked all the way through at the first stage. If you are not going to use cooked noodles straight away, toss them in a little oil to prevent them from sticking together or leave them to stand immersed in cold water. Noodles can be reheated by simply immersing them in hot water for a minute or so.

# types of noodles

# buckwheat and wheat noodles

Soba and green tea noodles are made from buckwheat flour and wheat flour in a ratio of about 4 to 1. Wheat noodles are made primarily from wheat flour and water; some have another ingredient such as sesame oil added. If you are cooking wheat noodles but are not serving them straight away, then toss them in a little oil to prevent them from sticking together.

### soba noodles

These are usually available as dried noodles. To cook, add the noodles to a large pan of boiling water, stirring to prevent them from sticking. Once the water has returned to the boil, add 1 cup of cold water. Cook for 6–8 minutes or until soft. Rinse under cold running water and drain well.

### instant noodles

These dried noodles have become extremely popular over the last 10 years because they are so convenient to use. Most brands require little or no preparation. For some you just add boiling water and allow to stand for a couple of minutes; others need to be cooked in boiling water for 2–5 minutes.

### wheat flour noodles

Also known as Shanghai, these noodles come in different widths and can be bought fresh or dried. Cook dried noodles in a large pan of boiling water (cooking time varies according the thickness of the noodles), then rinse under cold running water and drain. Add fresh noodles straight to the wok.

### green tea noodles

Green tea noodles, or cha soba as they are called in Japanese, are soba noodles that have powdered green tea added to the dough. They are an appealing bushy green colour with a subtle green tea flavour. Usually available dried, you can cook them in the same way as ordinary soba.

### udon noodles

Separate fresh udon before adding them to soups and stir-fries. If using them in salads, stand them in a bowl of boiling water for 2 minutes or until soft. Rinse under cold running water and drain well. Cook dried udon in a large pan of boiling water for 4–5 minutes or until soft. Rinse and drain.

### somen noodles

Somen noodles are dried, fine, white noodles made from wheat flour and cottonseed or sesame oil. Yellow tomago somen are enriched with egg yolk. To cook, place the noodles in a large pan of boiling water for 2–3 minutes or until soft, then rinse under cold running water and drain well.

# egg noodles

The Chinese call egg noodles dan mien. They are made from wheat flour and water and enriched with egg (from ducks or hens). In Thailand and Malaysia egg noodles are known as mee, in Indonesia they are called bakmi, in Vietnam they are referred to as mi and in Japan they are known as ramen. Most dried egg noodles can be fried to give a crisp noodle.

### dried egg noodles

Dried egg noodles come in different widths and are often bundled in skeins or clusters. As a general rule, one skein or cluster is enough for one serving. Cook the noodles in boiling water, following the cooking instructions on the packet, then rinse under cold running water and drain well.

### hokkien noodles

These fresh noodles are precooked. For stir-fries and soups, gently separate the strands of noodles and add them directly to the dishes. For salads, soften the noodles by standing them in a bowl of boiling water for 2 minutes. Rinse under cold running water and drain well.

### fresh egg noodles

Egg noodles are available in a variety of widths, from 1cm (½in) strands to thick strips. Cook them in a large pan of boiling water according to the instructions on the packet (around 2–3 minutes for thin noodles and 3–5 minutes for thick ones). Rinse under cold running water and drain well.

# rice and mung bean noodles

Extremely popular in Thailand, Malaysia, Vietnam and China, these noodles are made from rice flour and water. They are available in various forms, from fine vermicelli to wide ribbons and even noodle sheets. Rice noodles absorb a lot of moisture so, if you are substituting them for another type of noodle, you may need to increase the quantity of liquid used.

### fresh rice noodles

These fresh, precooked noodles should be kept at room temperature. If refrigerated, allow them to stand for 1 hour at room temperature before use. For soups and stir-fries, add the noodles directly to the wok and cook until heated through. Do not overcook or they will turn to mush.

### dried rice vermicelli

These are dried, fine, creamy-coloured noodles. For soups and salads, stand the noodles in boiling water for 10 minutes or until soft. Rinse under cold running water and drain well. For crisp noodles, cook the dried vermicelli in batches in hot oil until crisp and white. Drain on absorbent paper.

### dried glass noodles

These dried, fine noodles are made from mung bean starch and water. Stand the noodles in a bowl of boiling water for 5 minutes or until soft. Rinse under cold running water and drain well. To deep-fry, cook batches of the dried noodles in hot oil until puffed and white, then drain on absorbent paper.

### dried rice stick noodles

These dried noodles come in various widths. For soups and salads, stand the noodles in boiling water for 5–8 minutes or until soft. For stir-fries, stand them in boiling water for 3 minutes. Rinse under cold running water and drain well. Add to stir-fries with water or stock and cook until soft.

# soups & snacks

# chicken and vegetable noodle broth

Star anise gives this soup a wonderful Asian flavour. Select fragrant, firm stars. A good way to test their freshness is to break off a boat-shaped pod and squeeze it between your fingers until it pops – if it releases a warm aniseed smell, it is fresh.

300g (10½oz) dried instant
    noodles
1.5 litres (2½ pints) chicken
    stock
5cm (2in) piece of fresh ginger,
    thinly sliced
3 garlic cloves, sliced
¼ cup soy sauce
3 star anise
2 chicken breast fillets
1 bunch broccolini (long-
    stemmed broccoli) or purple
    sprouting broccoli, cut into
    3cm (1in) lengths
100g (3½oz) baby corn, halved
100g (3½oz) fresh shiitake
    mushrooms, sliced
2 spring onions, sliced

Preparation time: 15 minutes
Cooking time: 20 minutes
Serves: 4

Cook the instant noodles in boiling water for 3 minutes or until tender. Drain well.

Put the stock, ginger, garlic, soy and star anise into a saucepan and bring to the boil. Reduce the heat, add the chicken, then cover and simmer gently for 15 minutes or until the chicken is tender. Remove the chicken and allow it to cool slightly before shredding it into thin strips.

Add the broccolini, corn and mushrooms to the simmering stock and cook uncovered for 5 minutes or until the vegetables are soft.

Divide the noodles into four bowls, top with the soup and shredded chicken, then garnish with spring onions.

# udon broth with agedashi tofu

Silken firm tofu has a delightful junket-like texture that melts in the mouth. It is widely used in Japanese recipes, especially miso soup. Some brands can be watery and therefore need to be weighted and drained on absorbent paper for 10 minutes prior to use.

200g (7oz) dried somen noodles

300g (10½oz) silken firm tofu

corn flour, for dusting

1 teaspoon dashi granules

3 tablespoons light soy sauce

3 tablespoons mirin

oil, for deep-frying

2 tablespoons bonito flakes

Preparation time: 15 minutes

Cooking time: 10 minutes

Serves: 4

Cook the noodles in a large pan of boiling water for 2–3 minutes, or until soft, then rinse under cold running water, drain well and set aside.

Cut the tofu into 2cm (1in) thick squares and pat dry. Lightly dust both sides of the tofu with flour (the easiest way to turn the tofu is to use an egg flip).

Put the dashi granules, soy and mirin into a pan with 2 cups of water and bring to the boil. Reduce the heat and simmer for 5 minutes.

Heat the oil in a wok or pan. When hot, cook the tofu in batches until it is crisp and golden. Drain on absorbent paper.

Place a nest of noodles into four bowls and serve topped with deep-fried tofu and surrounded by broth. Sprinkle with bonito flakes.

# easy prawn laksa

Laksa originates in Malacca and is traditionally made using a blend of Malay spices simmered with prawns or chicken in coconut milk and finished with noodles. Singaporeans and inhabitants of southern Malaysia favour it as a mid-morning snack. It is also a great 'morning after' cure.

200g (7oz) dried rice vermicelli

1 tablespoon peanut oil

3–4 tablespoons laksa paste or
    red curry paste

750ml (1¼ pints) coconut milk

1 litre (1¾ pints) chicken stock

750g (1½lb) raw prawns,
    peeled, deveined, tails
    left intact

8 square tofu puffs,
    halved

100g (3½oz) bean sprouts

3 tablespoons fried Asian
    shallots

lime wedges and fresh herbs
    such as Vietnamese mint, to
    serve (optional)

Preparation time: 20 minutes

Cooking time: 20 minutes

Serves: 4

Put the noodles into a bowl, cover with boiling water and allow to soak for 10 minutes or until soft. Drain well.

Heat the oil in a large pan or wok, add the laksa paste and cook over a medium heat for 5 minutes or until fragrant.

Stir in the coconut milk and stock and bring to the boil. Reduce the heat to a simmer, add the prawns and tofu, and cook for 5 minutes or until the prawns are tender.

Divide the noodles and bean sprouts into four bowls, spoon the laksa over the top and serve sprinkled with Asian shallots. Serve with a wedge of lime and fresh herbs such as Vietnamese mint.

For a richer version of this recipe, substitute the chicken stock with another 750ml (1¼ pints) of coconut milk. If you would like to make a spicier soup, increase the quantity of laksa paste.

vietnamese beef noodle soup

prawn noodle toast

# vietnamese beef noodle soup

Eaten throughout Vietnam for breakfast, lunch or dinner, pho (pronounced fur) is the ultimate in comfort food. Fish sauce is a thin, salty liquid made from fermented fish. Although it does not sound appetizing, it gives another dimension to many Asian meals.

1.5 litres (2½ pints) good-
   quality beef stock
100g (3½oz) fresh ginger,
   peeled, sliced and bruised
2 cinnamon sticks
2 star anise
1 teaspoon black peppercorns
3 tablespoons fish sauce
600g (1¼lb) fresh rice noodles
100g (3½oz) bean sprouts
225g (8oz) beef fillet, very thinly
   sliced
coriander leaves, spring onions,
   lime wedges and finely
   cracked black pepper,
   to serve

Preparation time: 15 minutes
Cooking time: 20 minutes
Serves: 4

Put the stock, ginger, cinnamon, star anise and black peppercorns into a large pan and bring to the boil. Reduce the heat, cover and simmer for 20 minutes. Strain and discard the seasonings, return the stock to the pan and bring back to the boil.

Add the fish sauce to the stock. The degree of saltiness will vary from brand to brand, so it is a good idea to treat it like a seasoning, adding it a tablespoon at a time and tasting the stock until you achieve a flavour you like.

Divide the rice noodles, bean sprouts and thinly sliced beef into four bowls and ladle the stock over the top. Make sure that the stock is boiling before you pour it over the noodles because this is what will cook the beef.

Serve with coriander, spring onions, lime wedges and pepper, allowing each guest to add their own to the soup at the table.

# prawn noodle toast

This is a delicious twist on an old favourite. Be sure your bread is stale because fresh bread will absorb more oil and produce soggy toast. To test if the oil is hot enough to deep-fry, stand a wooden chopstick in the oil – if small bubbles appear around the chopstick, the oil is ready to use.

8 thick slices of day-old bread

750g (1½lb) raw medium-size
    prawns

2 eggs, separated

1 spring onion, thinly sliced

¼ teaspoon salt

¼ teaspoon white pepper

1 cup broken dried rice
    vermicelli

½ cup sesame seeds

oil, for deep-frying

sweet chilli sauce, for dipping

Preparation time: 25 minutes

Cooking time: 15 minutes

Makes: 16

Trim the crusts from the bread and discard them. Peel and devein the prawns, leaving 16 prawns with the tails intact.

Put the remaining prawns into a food processor with the egg whites, spring onion, salt and pepper and process to form a smooth paste.

Combine the crushed noodles and sesame seeds together. Spread one side of each slice of bread with the prawn mixture, then cut the bread in half. Top each half with a whole prawn. Brush the prawn and prawn paste lightly with egg yolk, then press into the combined crushed noodles and sesame seeds.

Heat the oil in a wok until hot, then deep-fry the prawn noodle toasts until crisp and golden brown. Drain on absorbent paper.

Serve with sweet chilli sauce for dipping.

# kumera ginger soup with sesame soba noodles

Miso comes in several different colours and flavours: as a general rule the lighter the colour, the sweeter the miso, the darker the more salty. Shiro miso, also known as white miso is great for soups and dressings—this is the one used for this recipe. Aka miso is a deep reddish brown colour and is excellent for miso soup.

500g (1lb) kumera (orange
    sweet potato), cubed
5cm (2in) piece of ginger,
    peeled and cut into
    thin slices
1 litre (1¾ pints) vegetable stock
1 tablespoon white miso
150g (5½oz) dried soba noodles
1 teaspoon sesame oil
3 spring onions, thinly sliced
2 tablespoons sesame seeds,
    toasted

Preparation time: 15 minutes
Cooking time: 25 minutes
Serves: 4

Put the kumera, ginger and stock into a saucepan and cook for 15 minutes or until the kumera is very soft.

Add the miso and cook for 3 minutes or until the miso dissolves, stirring continuously. Remove the ginger, then blend the soup in batches until smooth.

Add the soba noodles to a large pan of boiling water, stirring to prevent them from sticking. Once the water has returned to the boil, add 1 cup of cold water. Cook for 6–8 minutes or until soft. Rinse under cold running water and drain well.

Transfer the noodles to a bowl and toss through the sesame oil and spring onions. Serve the soup in shallow bowls topped with the noodles and a sprinkling of sesame seeds.

# crispy noodle and five spice nut mix

This recipe uses tamari, which is the name originally given to a rich dark soy sauce brewed with rice instead of wheat. This makes it a popular alternative to soy for people who have a gluten intolerance. However, these days some tamari brands do use wheat, so check the label if this is a concern for you.

100g (3½oz) thin dried egg
   noodles
oil, for shallow-frying
250g (8½oz) unsalted mixed
   nuts
100g (3½oz) rice cracker
   snack mix
1 teaspoon five spice powder
3 tablespoons tamari
1 teaspoon sesame oil

Preparation time: 10 minutes
Cooking time: 20 minutes
Makes: 3 cups

Preheat the oven to 180°C (350°F) or gas mark 4.

Shallow-fry batches of noodles in hot oil until they are crisp and golden, then drain on absorbent paper.

Put the nuts, snack mix, noodles, five spice powder, tamari and oil in a bowl and mix to combine.

Spread the nut mixture onto a non-stick baking tray lined with baking paper and bake for 15 minutes, turning it a couple of times during cooking, until the soy coating darkens and dries out.

Allow to cool and then serve as a snack with drinks. If you are not serving the noodle and nut mix straight away, store it in an airtight container.

# salmon noodle bonbons

Wonton wrappers come in two colours: yellow and white. The yellow ones contain food colouring and are made from a wheat-based dough. Traditionally, yellow wrappers are used for deep-fried wonton and white for steamed wontons. If you cannot find wonton wrappers, use spring roll wrappers cut into quarters.

12 wonton wrappers

300g (10½oz) salmon fillet cut
    from the centre of the fish

100g (3½oz) dried somen
    noodles

oil, for deep-frying

wasabi and soy sauce,
    for dipping

Preparation time: 20 minutes

Cooking time: 10 minutes

Makes: 12

Cut the wonton wrappers into 5cm (2in) wide pieces. Cut the salmon fillet into 2 x 5cm (1 x 2in) batons. Carefully break the noodles in half.

Lay out a small bunch of noodles on a flat surface and roll a piece of salmon over them, pressing lightly to ensure the noodles stick to the salmon.

Wrap each piece of noodle-coated salmon in a wonton wrapper and lightly brush the edge of the wrapper with water to secure.

Heat the oil in a wok until hot. Cook the bonbons in batches until crisp and golden. Drain on absorbent paper.

Serve with wasabi and soy dipping sauce.

duck noodle pancakes

vietnamese spring rolls

# duck noodle pancakes

The preparation required for making Chinese roast duck is fairly laborious so it is easier to buy the duck ready roasted. A good roast duck has a succulent but crisp skin. First, the duck is doused in boiling water several times and dried between each rinse. It is then glazed with a syrup mixture and strung up to dry before being roasted. Including a little of the crispy skin with the pancakes gives them extra flavour.

½ Chinese roast duck

50g (1¾oz) dried rice vermicelli

6 eggs, lightly beaten

2 teaspoons sherry

6 spring onions, thinly sliced

salt and pepper

2 teaspoons vegetable oil

150ml (¼ pint) chicken or duck
    stock

2 tablespoons palm sugar

1 tablespoon fish sauce

1 teaspoon sesame oil

Preparation time: 15 minutes

Cooking time: 20 minutes

Serves: 4

Remove the meat from the duck, taking care to keep the skin on the breast meat. Finely shred the rest of the flesh.

Put the noodles into a bowl, cover with boiling water and allow to stand for 10 minutes or until soft. Rinse and drain well.

Whisk together the eggs, sherry and half the spring onions and season generously with salt and pepper.

Pour ¼ cup of the mixture into a lightly oiled pan, then top with some noodles and shredded duck. Cook over a medium heat until the egg has set, then roll or fold up the sides of the set egg mixture to enclose the filling.

To make the broth, put the stock, sugar and fish sauce into a pan and bring to the boil. Remove from the heat and add the sesame oil.

Top the pancakes with some shredded duck and spring onions and drizzle over the broth.

# vietnamese spring rolls

Rice paper wrappers come in a variety of sizes and shapes, but large round or square wrappers are by far the easiest to roll. These spring rolls can be made in advance but must be stored in an airtight container layered with wet absorbent paper to prevent them from drying out. If you are short on time, you can always allow guests to prepare their own.

100g (3½oz) dried rice
    vermicelli
8 Chinese dried mushrooms
200g (7oz) firm tofu, diced
1 tablespoon grated fresh
    ginger
½ teaspoon five spice powder
1 cup grated carrot
⅓ cup small fresh mint leaves
12 round rice paper wrappers,
    each approximately 22cm
    (9in) in diameter
lemon juice
3 tablespoons hoisin sauce
½ tablespoon chilli sauce
oil, for deep-frying (optional)

Preparation time: 30 minutes
Cooking time: nil for fresh, 15 minutes for fried
Makes: 12

Put the noodles into a bowl, cover them with boiling water and allow to stand for 10 minutes or until soft. Rinse and drain well, then pat dry.

Put the mushrooms in a bowl, cover with ½ cup of boiling water and allow to stand for 10 minutes or until soft. Drain and reserve the liquid. Remove the stems from the mushrooms and cut the mushroom caps into fine slices.

Put the tofu, ginger and five spice into the mushroom liquid and allow to stand for 10 minutes to marinate. Drain and discard the liquid.

Put the noodles, carrot, mushrooms and mint into a bowl and gently mix to combine.

Soak one rice paper wrapper at a time in a little warm water with a squeeze of lemon juice until soft. Place the wrapper on a flat, dry surface and top with a heaped tablespoon of the noodle mixture and a few pieces of tofu. Roll up the wrapper, folding the sides in to form a spring roll shape.

Whisk together the hoisin and chilli sauces to make a dressing. Serve the spring rolls with the dressing. The rolls can be served fresh or deep fried in hot oil until crisp and golden.

# salads

# sesame and lime chicken noodle salad

When shopping for sesame oil you will find there are two colours: an amber-coloured oil and a darker brown oil. Both are made from crushed sesame seeds, but the darker oil uses toasted seeds and has a stronger flavour. The darker oil is used for cooking and seasoning; the lighter oil is generally used in dressings such as the one in this recipe.

200g (7oz) dried glass noodles

500g (1lb) chicken breast fillets

4 spring onions, sliced

2 carrots, thinly sliced

1 cucumber, thinly sliced

1 cup bean sprouts

1 cup coriander leaves

½ cup mint leaves

½ cup sesame seeds, toasted

2 tablespoons sweet chilli sauce

¼ cup lime juice

1 teaspoon light sesame oil

Preparation time: 20 minutes plus 10 minutes standing

Cooking time: 20 minutes

Serves: 4

Put the glass noodles into a bowl, cover with boiling water and allow to stand for 5 minutes or until the noodles are soft. Rinse under cold running water and drain well.

Steam the chicken over simmering water for 15 minutes or until tender. Allow to cool slightly, then shred.

Put the noodles, chicken, vegetables, herbs and sesame seeds into a bowl and mix to combine.

Whisk together the sweet chilli sauce, lime juice and sesame oil. Pour the dressing over the salad and toss to combine.

# crunchy cabbage, egg, almond and noodle salad

Deep-fried red Asian shallots are sold in jars in Asian food stores. Widely used in cooking throughout Asia, their sweet, intense onion flavour is an ideal ingredient for salads, stir-fries and soups. Sometimes they are sold as fried onions.

100g (3½oz) thin dried egg noodles

oil, for shallow-frying

200g (7oz) Chinese cabbage, finely shredded

100g (3½oz) flaked almonds, toasted

1 red pepper (capsicum), thinly sliced

1 large red chilli, thinly sliced

½ cup fried Asian shallots

4 hard-boiled eggs, roughly chopped

2 tablespoons fish sauce

2 tablespoons grated palm sugar

⅓ cup lemon juice

Preparation time: 15 minutes

Cooking time: 5 minutes

Serves: 4

Shallow-fry batches of noodles in hot oil until they are crisp and golden, then drain on absorbent paper.

Put the fried noodles, cabbage, almonds, red pepper, chilli and half the fried shallots into a bowl and toss to combine.

Arrange in mounds in four shallow bowls and top with chopped egg.

Whisk together the fish sauce, palm sugar and lemon juice and pour the dressing over the salad. Sprinkle with the remaining fried shallots before serving.

# pork, peanut and lemongrass noodle salad

Lemongrass is sold by the stalk. The tender white part of the stalk is used for cooking, while the green top may be bruised and added to soups and teas. The most important thing to remember when preparing lemongrass is that it needs to be finely chopped because it does not break down as it cooks. Growing lemongrass is very simple: stand the stalk in water, give it fresh water every day until it starts to sprout roots, then transfer it to a plant pot or the garden.

50g (1¾oz) dried glass noodles

125ml (4fl oz) coconut milk

2 tablespoons finely chopped
    lemongrass

500g (1lb) minced pork

3 tablespoons lime juice

2 tablespoons fish sauce

1 tablespoon grated palm sugar

½ cup chopped fresh mint

½ cup chopped roasted unsalted
    peanuts

baby cos lettuce, to serve

Preparation time: 15 minutes plus cooling

Cooking time: 15 minutes

Serves: 4–6

Put the glass noodles into a bowl and cover with boiling water. Allow to stand for 5 minutes or until the noodles are soft. Rinse under cold running water and drain well.

Heat a non-stick frying pan or wok, add the coconut milk, lemongrass and minced pork, and cook over a medium heat for 10 minutes or until the pork is tender. Drain off any excess liquid. Transfer to a bowl and allow to cool.

Whisk together the lime juice, fish sauce and palm sugar. Add the noodles to the mince and pour over the dressing. Stir to combine. Fold through the mint and peanuts and serve in baby cos lettuce leaves.

# sticky pork and mango noodle salad

Hoisin sauce is probably best known as the tangy brown sauce served with Peking duck. It is a combination of sugar, garlic, spices and fermented soy beans and is the perfect accompaniment to pork. Widely used in Chinese cooking, it is available in Asian food stores.

4 boneless pork spare ribs

2 tablespoons plum sauce

2 tablespoons hoisin sauce

400g (14oz) fresh hokkien
    noodles

2 spring onions, sliced

1 red pepper (capsicum), thinly
    sliced

1 large mango, thinly sliced

Preparation time: 20 minutes

Cooking time: 20 minutes

Serves: 4

Trim the skin and bones from the pork ribs and place on a grill tray lined with aluminium foil. Combine the plum and hoisin sauces and brush the mixture over one side of the ribs. Cook under a preheated grill for 5 minutes or until the glaze is bubbling. Turn over the ribs and baste the other side, then cook for another 5 minutes or until the pork it tender. Allow to cool slightly, then slice into thin strips.

Put the noodles into a bowl, cover with boiling water and allow to stand for 2 minutes or until heated through. Drain well.

Put the pork, noodles, spring onions, pepper and mango into a bowl and toss gently to combine.

# stacked soba and spinach salad

The Chinese introduced soy sauce to the Japanese. Early in the 15th century, the Japanese began producing their own varieties to suit their style of food. Japanese soy contains more wheat than its Chinese counterparts, is usually aged for up to six months and is generally sweeter and less salty.

200g (7oz) dried soba noodles

2 tablespoons sesame seeds, toasted

1 tablespoon caster sugar

3 tablespoons Japanese soy sauce

60ml (2fl oz) vegetable stock, chilled

½ teaspoon sesame oil

500g (1lb) spinach

Preparation time: 15 minutes

Cooking time: 10 minutes

Serves: 4

Add the soba noodles to a large pan of boiling water, stirring to prevent them from sticking. Once the water has returned to the boil, add 1 cup of cold water. Cook for 6–8 minutes or until soft. Drain and transfer to a bowl of iced water to cool while you prepare the dressing.

Lightly grind 1 tablespoon of the sesame seeds in a mortar and pestle, then transfer to a bowl. Stir in the sugar, soy, stock and sesame oil and whisk to combine.

Cook the spinach in boiling water until tender, then rinse under cold water and cut in half.

Stack the drained noodles onto a plate, top with the spinach (one half of the spinach stacked on top of the other half) and drizzle the dressing over the top. Sprinkle the remaining sesame seeds on top.

# warm lemon squid noodle salad

Although technically not a member of the mint family, Vietnamese mint is a pungent herb with a heady mint aroma. Also known as laksa leaf or hot mint, its elongated leaves have a hint of purple that runs either side of the centre. If you cannot find Vietnamese mint leaves, use ordinary mint leaves instead.

150g (5½oz) dried rice vermicelli

500g (1lb) fresh squid tubes
   (smaller is better)

sea salt

2 small onions, thinly sliced

1 small red chilli, thinly sliced

2 garlic cloves, crushed

60ml (2fl oz) lemon juice

1 tablespoon caster sugar

1 cup small, fresh, Vietnamese
   mint leaves

1 tablespoon finely shredded
   lemon zest

Preparation time: 15 minutes plus cooling

Cooking time: 10 minutes

Serves: 4

Put the rice vermicelli into a bowl, cover with boiling water and allow to stand for 10 minutes or until soft. Drain well.

Cut the squid into thin strips. Put the squid and a pinch of sea salt into a frying pan and cook over a medium–high heat for 2 minutes or until the squid turns white.

Add the onion, chilli and garlic and cook for 3 minutes or until the onion is soft. Transfer to a chilled bowl and allow to cool.

Whisk together the lemon and sugar and pour the dressing over the squid. Add the mint leaves, lemon zest and noodles and toss gently to combine.

# spicy coconut beef and noodle salad

Not knowing how to crack open a coconut is often the reason many people do not buy one. However, the process is simple. Push a skewer through the eyes at the bottom of the coconut and drain out the liquid. Bake the coconut in a hot oven for 15 minutes, then hit it around the centre with a hammer until it splits open.

250g (8½oz) thick dried wheat
  flour noodles
1–2 tablespoons madras curry
  paste
2 teaspoons grated palm sugar
500g (1lb) rump steak
1 cup coconut cream
1 tablespoon fish sauce
½ cup shaved fresh coconut or
  flaked coconut
100g (3½oz) baby spinach
  leaves
300g (10½oz) orange sweet
  potatoes, sliced and
  steamed
¼ tablespoon chopped fresh
  mint

Preparation time: 25 minutes
Cooking time: 15 minutes
Serves: 4

Cook the noodles in a large pan of rapidly boiling water for 5–10 minutes or until tender. Rinse under cold water and drain well.

Combine the curry paste and 1 teaspoon of the sugar and generously baste both sides of the beef.

Cook on a preheated chargrill plate for 3 minutes each side or until medium-rare. The cooking time may vary slightly, depending on the thickness of the steak. Allow to rest for 5 minutes, then cut into thin strips across the grain.

Put the coconut cream, fish sauce and remaining palm sugar into a bowl and whisk to combine.

Put the noodles, fresh or flaked coconut, spinach, sweet potato and half the mint into a bowl and toss to combine. Divide the mixture onto four plates, top with the beef and serve drizzled with the coconut dressing. Sprinkle the remaining mint on top.

sashimi noodle salad

chilli duck and pineapple noodle salad

# sashimi noodle salad

The Japanese use pickled ginger (gari) as a condiment served with sushi. It is available in a variety of colours, from white to blushing pink through to bright red. The young ginger roots are lightly salted and then marinated in a sweetened rice vinegar mixture, which gives the ginger its pinkish colour. However, some brands use food colouring to achieve a more vibrant colour.

250g (8½oz) dried green tea
   noodles
300g (10½oz) sashimi tuna
1 avocado, sliced
1 small cucumber, sliced
2 tablespoons pickled ginger
⅓ cup seasoned rice vinegar
1 tablespoon soy sauce
1 tablespoon black sesame seeds

Preparation time: 15 minutes
Cooking time: 10 minutes
Serves: 4

Add the green tea noodles to a large pan of boiling water, stirring to prevent them from sticking. Once the water has returned to the boil, add 1 cup of cold water. Cook for 6–8 minutes or until soft. Transfer to a bowl of iced water and allow to cool for 5 minutes.

Cut the tuna into 5mm (¼in) thick slices.

Arrange the noodles into nests in four shallow bowls. Place the avocado, cucumber, pickled ginger and tuna on top.

Whisk together the rice vinegar and soy sauce in a bowl. Drizzle the mixture over the salad and garnish with black sesame seeds.

# chilli duck and pineapple noodle salad

Chinese rice vinegar is widely used in Asian cuisine. It is a clear, slightly sweet vinegar made from fermented rice. If you have trouble finding it, use diluted white wine or cider vinegar instead.

400g (14oz) fresh hokkien
noodles, separated
1 Chinese roast duck cut into
bite-size pieces, or 3 roasted
duck breasts
2 tomatoes, cut into wedges
100g (3½oz) mangetout (snow
peas)
300g (10½oz) fresh pineapple,
cut into wedges
4 spring onions, thinly sliced
1 teaspoon chilli oil
3 tablespoons plum sauce
3 tablespoons Chinese rice
vinegar

Preparation time: 15 minutes
Cooking time: nil
Serves: 4

Put the hokkien noodles into a bowl, cover with boiling water and allow to stand for 2 minutes or until just tender. Rinse under cold running water and drain well.

Put the noodles, duck, tomatoes, mangetout, pineapple and spring onions into a bowl.

Whisk together the chilli oil, plum sauce and vinegar in a bowl and pour over the salad. Gently toss to coat.

# crispy prawn summer noodle salad

Thai cooking uses large red chillies to add colour to dishes rather than heat. Removing the seeds and membrane will take away most of the bite from these chillies. If you prefer more of a kick, however, use small bird's eye chillies.

500g (1lb) medium prawns,
    cooked
oil, for shallow-frying
100g (3½oz) dried glass noodles,
    separated
1 green apple, cut into julienne
    strips
1 carrot, cut into julienne strips
1 tomato, deseeded and cut
    into thin strips
1 large red chilli, deseeded and
    cut into thin strips
2 spring onions, thinly sliced
1–2 tablespoons fish sauce
3 tablespoons lemon juice
2 teaspoons palm sugar

Preparation time: 30 minutes
Cooking time: 20 minutes
Serves: 4

Peel and devein the prawns, leaving the tails intact.

Heat the oil in a wok or shallow frying pan until hot. Add the separated glass noodles in batches and cook until they puff and turn white. Drain on absorbent paper.

Put the prawns, apple, carrot, tomato, chilli and spring onion into a bowl and toss gently to combine.

Whisk together the fish sauce, lemon juice and palm sugar and pour the resulting mixture over the salad. Gently toss to combine.

# stir-fries

# creamy peanut noodles with lamb satay sticks

Kecap manis is a thick sweet Indonesian soy sauce. There are different types available, from sweet through to slightly salty. This recipe uses the sweet variety; if you have trouble finding it, substitute soy mixed with honey.

500g (1lb) lamb loin, cut into
    thin strips
2 tablespoons kecap manis
400g (14oz) fresh hokkien
    noodles, separated
1 tablespoon peanut oil
1 onion, finely chopped
4 tablespoons peanut butter
1½ cups coconut cream
1 tablespoon sweet chilli sauce
1 tablespoon lemon juice
2 tablespoons fresh coriander
    sprigs

Preparation time: 25 minutes plus 30 minutes marinating
Cooking time: 20 minutes
Serves: 4

Place the lamb and kecap manis into a non-metallic bowl and allow to stand for 30 minutes.

Put the separated noodles into a bowl and cover with boiling water. Allow to stand for 2 minutes or until soft.

Thread the lamb onto bamboo skewers and cook under a preheated grill for 3–5 minutes or until tender. Keep warm.

Heat the oil in a wok, add the onion and cook over a medium heat for 5 minutes or until golden. Add the peanut butter, coconut cream, sweet chilli sauce and lemon juice and cook, stirring continuously, until the sauce boils and thickens slightly. Toss the cooked mixture through the noodles and garnish with coriander just before serving.

Serve the noodles in bowls, accompanied by the satay sticks.

# spiced turmeric fish with fresh herbs and noodles

Although it is not commonly known, there are two types of turmeric powder: Madras and Alleppey. Madras is the vibrant light yellow powder that has long been used in recipes all around the world. Preferred by some people for its mild flavour, it is often used in curries and condiments. Alleppey is several shades darker and has a stronger flavour. This recipe will work using either.

200g (7oz) dried rice stick
   noodles
2 tablespoons vegetable oil
3 teaspoons turmeric powder
1 tablespoon grated fresh
   ginger
500g (1lb) firm white fish fillets
   such as cod, sea bass or
   monkfish, cut into 2cm
   (1in) cubes
2 tablespoons fish sauce
1 tablespoon sugar
¼ cup chicken stock
3 tablespoons chopped fresh dill
6 spring onions, cut into 5cm
   (2in) pieces
⅓ cup roasted unsalted
   peanuts

Preparation time: 10 minutes
Cooking time: 15 minutes
Serves: 4

Put the rice stick noodles into a bowl and cover with boiling water. Allow to stand for 5–8 minutes or until soft. Drain well.

Heat the oil in a large frying pan, add the turmeric and ginger and cook over a medium heat for 3 minutes or until fragrant.

Add the fish, fish sauce, sugar and stock and cook for 5 minutes or until the fish is tender. Remove from the heat and stir through the dill, spring onions and noodles.

Divide the noodles into four bowls and serve with a side dish of peanuts.

# stir-fried rice noodles with chicken and basil

Thai basil is also known as horapa, Asian sweet basil and cinnamon basil. It has a strong, heady and slightly mentholated fragrance and is probably best known as the herb used in Thai curries and stir-fries. The easiest way to distinguish Thai basil from other types is by its purple stem and a purplish tinge at the top of the leaf. If it is not available, substitute ordinary basil.

500g (1lb) chicken breast fillets,
    sliced
2 tablespoons fish sauce
3 tablespoons oyster sauce
3 teaspoons sugar
1 cup Thai basil leaves
2 tablespoons soy bean oil
4 garlic cloves, crushed
2 small red chillies, deseeded
    and thinly sliced
500g (1lb) fresh rice noodles

Preparation time: 10 minutes plus 10 minutes marinating
Cooking time: 10 minutes
Serves: 4

Put the chicken, fish sauce, oyster sauce, sugar and half the basil leaves into a non-metallic bowl, and set aside to marinate for 10 minutes.

Heat the oil in a wok, add the garlic and chilli and stir-fry over a medium heat for 2 minutes or until the garlic is fragrant.

Add the chicken and stir-fry for 5 minutes or until tender. Add the noodles and stir-fry for 2 minutes or until heated through.

Toss through the remaining basil leaves just before serving.

quick pad thai

tangy sweet-and-sour tofu and vegetables with noodles

# quick pad thai

Tofu, also known as bean curd, comes in several varieties. Soft or silken tofu is fragile and usually steamed or added to soups. Firm or hard tofu and silken firm tofu are more solid and can be sliced and added to stir-fries without breaking up. The tofu sold in health food stores is usually the hard variety and is therefore suitable for this recipe.

1 tablespoon soy bean oil

4 small garlic cloves, crushed

300g (10½oz) firm tofu, cut
    into 1cm (½in) strips

2 eggs, lightly beaten

3 tablespoons fish sauce

3 teaspoons sugar

1 cup warm water

200g (7oz) dried rice stick
    noodles, soaked in warm
    water for 2 minutes

2 tablespoons ground peanuts

2 tablespoons dried shrimp

2 spring onions, sliced

2 tablespoons lime juice

lime wedges, to serve

Preparation time: 15 minutes

Cooking time: 10 minutes

Serves: 4

Heat the oil in a wok, add the garlic and tofu and stir-fry over a medium heat for 5 minutes or until the tofu is golden.

Add the egg, fish sauce and sugar and stir-fry until the egg is scrambled. Push the egg up one side of the wok and add the water and noodles. Gently stir for 5 minutes or until the noodles soften.

Add the peanuts, shrimp and spring onion and stir-fry the whole mixture for 2 minutes to heat through.

Remove from the heat and season to taste with the lime juice. Serve with wedges of lime.

# tangy sweet-and-sour tofu and vegetables with noodles

The Chinese have been making sweet-and-sour dishes for centuries. The sauce is usually thickened with cornflour and can have a cloying quality. This Thai-style sauce is not thickened and is less sweet than the Chinese version. If you would prefer a thicker sauce, mix 2 teaspoons of cornflour into the sauce before adding it to the wok.

1 tablespoon vegetable oil

4 small garlic cloves, crushed

1 small onion, sliced

200g (7oz) firm tofu, cubed

1 carrot, sliced

1 red pepper (capsicum), sliced

100g (3½oz) baby corn, halved

100g (3½oz) mangetout (snow peas)

250g (8½oz) fresh pineapple, cut into bite-size wedges

1 firm tomato, cut into thin wedges

6 tablespoons lime juice

6 tablespoons sugar

2 tablespoons soy sauce

200g (7oz) thin fresh egg noodles

**Preparation time: 10 minutes**

**Cooking time: 10 minutes**

**Serves: 4**

Heat the oil in a wok and add the garlic, onion and tofu. Stir-fry over a medium heat for 3 minutes or until the garlic is fragrant and the onion soft.

Add the carrot, pepper, corn, mangetout, pineapple and tomato and stir-fry for 2 minutes.

Whisk together the lime juice, sugar and soy sauce. Stir the liquid into the vegetables and bring to the boil.

Cook the noodles in a large pan of boiling water for 3–5 minutes or until tender, then rinse and drain.

Divide the noodles between four bowls and top with the vegetables.

# udon noodle nests with teriyaki chicken

Mirin is golden-coloured, sweetened rice wine that is often used in Japanese cooking. Its low alcohol content is burned off during cooking, while its high sugar content gives grilled foods and basting sauces an attractive glossy finish. Look for hon mirin because this is the best quality.

300g (10½oz) dried udon
   noodles
1 tablespoon oil
500g (1lb) chicken thigh fillets,
   cut into 3cm (1in) thick strips
1 bunch of asparagus, cut into
   5cm (2in) lengths
1 teaspoon cornflour
2 tablespoons sake
2 tablespoons mirin
2 tablespoons soy sauce
1 teaspoons sugar

Preparation time: 10 minutes
Cooking time: 10 minutes
Serves: 4

Cook the udon noodles in a large pan of boiling water for 4–5 minutes or until tender. Drain well.

Heat the oil in a wok, add the chicken and stir-fry over a medium heat for 5 minutes or until tender. Add the asparagus and stir-fry for 2 minutes or until bright green.

Whisk together the cornflour and a little of the sake to form a paste, then add the remaining sake, mirin, soy sauce and sugar and stir until smooth. Pour into the wok, and stir until the sauce boils and thickens slightly.

Serve the chicken on nests of noodles.

# caramelized pepper pork noodles

Palm sugar is sold in many forms: flat round cakes, solid tubes and also in jars. It is made from the sap of the sugar palm. The sap is heated and poured into moulds, and varies in colour from light caramel to dense brown. It is widely used in both savoury and sweet dishes in southeast Asian cooking.

300g (10½oz) thick fresh egg
   noodles
½ cup palm sugar
⅔ cup fish sauce
1 teaspoon cracked black
   pepper
1 teaspoon five spice powder
500g (1lb) pork fillet, sliced
250g (8½oz) broccoli, cut into
   florets

Preparation time: 15 minutes
Cooking time: 20 minutes
Serves: 4

Cook the noodles in boiling water for 3–5 minutes. Rinse under cold running water and drain well.

Put the sugar into a wok and cook over a low heat until the sugar dissolves. Slowly stir in the fish sauce and bring to the boil. Cook over a medium heat for 10 minutes or until the sauce is thick and caramelized.

Add the pepper, five spice powder and pork fillet, cover and simmer for 5 minutes or until the pork is tender.

Add the broccoli and cook for 3 minutes or until bright green and tender.

Add the noodles to the caramelized pork and stir-fry for 2 minutes to heat through.

# green tea noodles with tofu and soy butter

Soy beans are renowned for being the most highly nutritious of all beans and for this reason they have become a staple of the Asian community. The same type of bean is used for cooking, drying and making soy sauce, tofu, milk and miso.

200g (7oz) dried green tea
    noodles
1 tablespoon vegetable oil
1 tablespoon finely grated
    fresh ginger
300g (10½oz) firm tofu, cut
    into 2cm (1in) cubes
100g (3½oz) frozen soy beans
3 tablespoons soy sauce
2 tablespoons mirin
50g (1¾oz) butter

Preparation time: 15 minutes
Cooking time: 15 minutes
Serves: 4

Add the noodles to a large pan of boiling water, stirring to prevent them from sticking. Once the water has returned to the boil, add 1 cup of cold water. Cook for 6–8 minutes or until soft. Rinse the noodles under cold water and drain well.

Heat the oil in a wok, add the ginger and tofu and stir-fry over a medium heat for 5 minutes or until the tofu is golden brown.

Add the beans, soy sauce and mirin and simmer for 3 minutes or until the beans are soft. Whisk in the butter.

Arrange the noodles in nests in four bowls. Top the noodles with the tofu mixture.

singapore street noodles

egg noodles with oriental mushrooms

# singapore street noodles

The most popular Chinese rice wine is sold as shao hsing or shao xing, a gorgeous clear amber liquid. It is preferred over other brands because it is aged for up to 10 years. If you cannot locate it, dry sherry is a good substitute. Traditionally, rice wine is purchased on the birth of a daughter and stored until she is married.

500g (1lb) chicken thigh fillets,
   thinly sliced
4 tablespoons Chinese rice wine
   or dry sherry
2 tablespoons soy sauce
2 teaspoons cornflour
2 teaspoons vegetable oil
1 red pepper (capsicum), thinly
   sliced
600g (1¼lb) fresh hokkien
   noodles, separated
100g (3½oz) bean sprouts
2 tablespoons garlic chives,
   chopped

Preparation time: 15 minutes
Cooking time: 15 minutes
Serves: 4

Put the chicken, rice wine, soy sauce and cornflour into a bowl and mix to combine. Allow to marinate for 10 minutes.

Heat the oil in a wok, add the chicken mix and stir-fry over a medium–high heat for 5 minutes or until tender.

Add the pepper and stir-fry for 1 minute or until soft.

Add the noodles, bean sprouts and chives and stir-fry until heated through.

# egg noodles with oriental mushrooms

Fresh shiitake mushrooms have a mild, woody mushroom flavour that intensifies with age. First grown in Japan, they are known as the king of the mushrooms because they are believed to increase longevity. Remove the hard stem and thinly slice the caps. Substitute dried shiitake if fresh are not available, and use the soaking liquid to add extra flavour to the sauce.

200g (7oz) thin dried egg
    noodles
2 tablespoons soy bean oil
3 garlic cloves, crushed
150g (5¼oz) fresh shiitake
    mushrooms, sliced
150g (5¼oz) oyster mushrooms
100g (3½oz) enoki mushrooms
3 tablespoons kecap manis
    (sweet soy sauce)
4 tablespoons mushroom oyster
    sauce
2 tablespoons fresh garlic chives,
    snipped

Preparation time: 15 minutes
Cooking time: 15 minutes
Serves: 4

Cook the noodles in a large pan of boiling water for 2–3 minutes or until tender. Rinse under cold water and drain well.

Heat the oil in a wok, add the garlic and the shiitake and oyster mushrooms and stir-fry over a medium heat for 3 minutes or until the mushrooms are brown and all the liquid has evaporated.

Add the enoki mushrooms, kecap manis and mushroom oyster sauce and bring to the boil. Add a couple of tablespoons of water if the sauce is too thick.

Spoon the noodles into four bowls and top with the mushrooms.

# chargrilled chicken breast topped with green curry noodles

Coconut milk is made by soaking grated fresh or desiccated coconut in hot water. The thickness of the milk varies from brand to brand and it can be hard to tell the difference between the coconut cream and milk. Coconut milk should be liquid and the cream should have a thick, solidified layer on top when you open the can.

200g (7oz) thick dried rice stick
noodles
200g (7oz) green beans, sliced
4 small chicken breast fillets
1 tablespoon vegetable oil
1 tablespoon green curry paste
4 kaffir lime leaves, finely
shredded
400ml (14fl oz) coconut milk
1 tablespoon fish sauce
1 tablespoon palm sugar

Preparation time: 15 minutes
Cooking time: 20 minutes
Serves: 4

Put the noodles in a large bowl and cover with boiling water. Allow to stand for 5–8 minutes. Rinse under cold water and drain well. Steam the beans until tender.

Trim any excess fat and sinew from the chicken breasts. Heat 2 teaspoons of the oil in a chargrill pan, add the chicken and cook over a medium–high heat for 10–15 minutes, turning once, until the chicken is tender. Allow to cool slightly and then cut into thin slices.

Heat the remaining oil in a wok, add the curry paste and kaffir lime leaves and stir-fry over a medium heat for 2 minutes or until the curry paste is fragrant. Add the coconut milk and cook for 3 minutes. Season with the fish sauce and sugar.

Serve mounds of the noodles topped with some of the curry sauce, green beans, slices of chicken and the rest of the sauce.

# garlic, pepper and lemongrass beef with noodles

The easiest way to distinguish Chinese broccoli (gai larn) from other Asian greens is by the small white flowers. Choy sum is almost identical but has yellow flowers, and can easily be used as a substitute. Roughly chop the leaves and tender young stalks before steaming or adding to soups and stir-fries. Gai larn is an excellent source of calcium for vegetarians.

400g (14oz) instant noodles

3 lemongrass stalks (white part
   only), thinly sliced

4 garlic cloves, roughly chopped

½ teaspoon white pepper

4 tablespoons fish sauce

4 teaspoons honey

500g (1lb) rump steak, cut into
   thin strips

1 tablespoon oil

1 bunch Chinese broccoli,
   roughly chopped

Preparation time: 20 minutes plus 15 minutes marinating

Cooking time: 10 minutes

Serves: 4

Cook the noodles in boiling water following the instructions on the packet, then rinse under cold running water, drain well and set aside.

Put the lemongrass, garlic and pepper into a mortar and pestle or spice grinder and pound or blend to form a smooth paste. Transfer to a non-metallic bowl, add the fish sauce, honey and steak and allow to marinate for 15 minutes. The longer you leave the beef in the marinade, the stronger the flavour will be.

Heat the oil in a wok, add the beef along with marinade and stir-fry over a high heat for 5 minutes or until browned. Remove.

Add the Chinese broccoli and 2 tablespoons of water. Stir-fry for 2 minutes or until bright green and tender.

Toss the noodles through the greens and stir-fried beef.

# sweet chilli pumpkin and cashew noodles

Sweet chilli sauce is extremely popular in Thailand, where it is used as an accompaniment to fried foods. The heat of the sauce varies from brand to brand, but even the hotter varieties are, as the name suggests, more sweet than fiery.

200g (7oz) dried rice vermicelli

1 tablespoon vegetable oil

1 tablespoon grated fresh
    ginger

750g (1½lb) butternut pumpkin
    (squash), cut into 2cm (1in)
    cubes

½ cup water

⅓ cup sweet chilli sauce

1 tablespoon lemon juice

125g (4½oz) cashews, roasted

2 tablespoons roughly chopped
    fresh coriander leaves

Preparation time: 15 minutes

Cooking time: 30 minutes

Serves: 4

Put the vermicelli in a bowl, cover with boiling water and allow to stand for 10 minutes or until soft. Rinse under cold water and drain well.

Heat the oil in a wok, add the ginger and pumpkin and cook over a medium heat for 5 minutes or until the pumpkin starts to brown. Add the water, cover and cook for 10 minutes or until the pumpkin is soft.

Increase the heat and stir in the sweet chilli sauce and lemon juice. Bring to the boil and cook until the sauce is thick and sticky. Toss through the noodles, cashews and coriander.

barbecue pork with asian greens

prawn and scallop noodles

# barbecue pork with asian greens

Choy sum is sometimes called Chinese flowering cabbage. It has bright yellow flowers and a subtle mustard flavour. It is suitable for steaming, stir-frying or adding to soups. Char sui pork is also known as red roast pork and can be seen hanging in the windows of Chinese barbecue kitchens all around the world. The pork has been marinated in hoisin, spices, sugar and soy before being roasted.

1 tablespoon oil

4 spring onions, sliced

500g (1lb) char sui pork, thickly sliced

500g (1lb) choy sum, roughly chopped

500g (1lb) fresh wheat flour noodles

3 tablespoons soy sauce

3 tablespoons hoisin sauce

Preparation time: 10 minutes

Cooking time: 10 minutes

Serves: 4

Heat the oil in a wok, add the spring onions and barbecue pork and stir-fry over a medium heat for 5 minutes or until the pork is tender.

Add the choy sum and stir-fry for 2 minutes until the leaves soften. Add the noodles, stir in the sauces (after first combining them) and cook until the sauce boils and thickens.

# prawn and scallop noodles

Oyster sauce is a thick salty brown sauce made by simmering oysters in salt water and soy sauce. The Cantonese use it as an all-purpose seasoning for meat, fish, vegetables and noodles. It has a mild flavour that is not very oyster-like at all. Select a brand that includes premium oyster extract in its list of ingredients for optimum flavour.

750g (1½lb) medium raw
    prawns
200g (7oz) scallops
1 tablespoon vegetable oil
1 onion, sliced into thin wedges
1 teaspoon five spice powder
150g (5¼oz) sugar snap peas
1 bunch baby bok choy, roughly
    chopped
400g (14oz) fresh udon noodles,
    separated
3 tablespoons oyster sauce
2 tablespoons soy sauce
2 tablespoons honey

Preparation time: 15 minutes
Cooking time: 10 minutes
Serves: 4

Peel and devein the prawns, leaving the tails intact. Remove the roe from the scallops.

Heat the oil in a wok, add the prawns and stir-fry over a medium–high heat for 3 minutes or until the prawns turn pink. Add the scallops and cook for another 2 minutes. Remove the prawns and scallops from the wok and set them aside.

Add the onion, five spice powder and 2 tablespoons of water to the wok. Cook over a medium–high heat for 3 minutes or until soft.

Add the sugar snap peas, bok choy and noodles. Stir-fry for 2 minutes or until the noodles are soft.

Combine the oyster sauce, soy sauce and honey then stir the mixture in, cooking it until it is heated through.

# glossary & index

# ingredients glossary

## asian greens

There is a large variety of these greens available in Asian supermarkets – details of the three most common are given below. They all require very little cooking and are best served slightly crisp. They can all be substituted for each other.

bok choy – also known as pak choy, has a very mild mustard flavour, it can be added to soups and stir-fries or may be steamed.

choy sum – also known as Chinese flowering cabbage, is easily recognized by its yellow flowers. It is often served in Chinese restaurants, steamed and topped with oyster sauce.

gai larn – this has white flowers, but in every other detail is just like choy sum.

## curry paste

green curry – made using fresh green chillies and spices. This is milder than red curry paste though different brands will vary in pungency.

laksa – this is a spicy paste made by combining red chillies, shrimp paste, lemongrass and spices. It is not usually as hot as red curry paste. Substitute red paste in small quantities if laksa is not available.

red curry – made from dried chillies and spices, this is usually hotter than green curry paste so use sparingly.

## fish sauce

This clear brown sauce is made from salted and fermented dried fish. It is widely used in Thailand and Vietnam as a seasoning, and has a pungent salty taste. Its flavour is distinctive, but if it is not available try seasoning with a little soy sauce instead. (Remember that soy will change the colour of curries so you may want to use a little extra salt instead.)

## fried shallots

Sold in jars or bags in Asian supermarkets, these are golden brown-coloured fried red shallots. If they are not available you can make your own by shallow-frying thinly sliced shallots.

## hoisin

This sweet reddish brown sauce is used for Peking duck. If it is not available substitute plum sauce, though this is a little sweeter so you may want to adjust the amount accordingly.

## kaffir lime leaves

These are shiny green citrus flavoured leaves that are widely used in Thai cooking. If they are not available you can use dried kaffir lime leaves or fresh lemon or lime leaves instead.

## mirin

A low alcohol rice wine with a high sugar content, this is used in marinades and sauces to provide a glossy sheen. If unavailable substitute with a sweet sherry.

## mushrooms

enoki – these are miniature long-stemmed white mushrooms that are sold in clumps. They cook in seconds so add just before serving. Remove the solid root base before cooking.

oyster – these mushrooms are oyster-shaped and have feathery gills. They have a subtle mushroom flavour and are best used in stir-fries.

shiitake – these mushrooms are available fresh or dried; the fresh have a strong mushroom flavour and make a great addition to stir-fries. The dried ones are sometimes sold as Chinese mushrooms so look for examples with a diamond pattern on the top of their cap. Rehydrate them in boiling water, then remove the stalks and slice the caps. The soaking liquid also has a delicious flavour and can be added to soups and sauces. If fresh ones are not available, you can substitute with any other mushrooms.

## palm sugar

This firm sugar is made from the sticky sap of the palm tree. It comes in two colours, pale golden and dark brown, and is sold in jars, flat round cakes or cylindrical tubes. The sugar is quite difficult to remove from the jar, so look for the cakes or tubes and use a sharp knife to shave off shards as when you need them.

### pickled ginger

This is thinly sliced ginger that has been left to soak in vinegar until it turns pink. It is easy to make your own.

### rice vinegar

This vinegar is made from fermented white rice – if it is not available then substitute a mild white vinegar. Japanese rice vinegar differs slightly from Chinese but they can be substituted for each other. Japanese-seasoned rice vinegar has had sugar and seasoning added so that it may be placed directly in rice to make sushi rice.

### sake

Japanese rice wine used for cooking, sake has a high alcohol content so must be brought to the boil to evaporate the alcohol. Do not use white wine instead as its flavour is too strong.

### soy sauce

Asian cooking uses soy sauce where the West uses salt. There are many different shades and strengths of soy sauce – Kikkoman is the best-known brand.

dark and light soy – dark soy is used as a seasoning for stronger-flavoured dishes such as hot pots and meat and pork dishes. Light soy is used for seafood, vegetables and stir-fries.

japanese soy – this is not sold as 'Japanese soy' but the bottles usually display Japanese writing. This is best suited to Japanese-style cooking, as it is a little less salty then Chinese soy.

kecap manis – this is a thick sweet soy used in Indonesian cooking. If it is not available then substitute with soy sauce and a little honey.

tamari – this soy sauce is made with rice instead of wheat. If it is not available Japanese soy will substitute.

### star anise

This small star-shaped spice has a soft sweet aniseed/liquorice taste and fragrance and it is often used to flavour Asian soups and stocks. Whole stars that are stored in an airtight container should keep for a year or so.

### sweet chilli sauce

This mild, sweet chilli-flavoured sauce is widely used in Thai cooking. It is mainly served as a dipping sauce, but also makes a delicious addition to marinades and stir-fries as it is not too spicy. If it is not available then substitute a mild chilli sauce mixed with a little honey.

### tofu

Sold in a variety of forms, tofu is also known as bean curd. Below is a general guideline to the different types that are available. It is advisable to take a close look at the texture in the shop as often they will vary depending on the brand. Japanese tofu is usually softer than Chinese tofu and tofu sold in health stores is usually more solid.

deep-fried tofu – these large cubes of tofu that have been deep-fried can be added to soups. Their spongy texture absorbs the soup's flavours.

firm tofu – this usually has a more solid, rubbery texture and can therefore withstand both marinating and barbecuing.

silken firm tofu – as the name suggests, this is a little firmer than silken tofu so it can be cooked without it crumbling.

silken tofu – this soft, custard-like curd is very fragile and requires virtually no cooking at all. It is often diced and then added to miso soup.
*Note:* Most silken, silken firm and firm tofu is sold in containers immersed in water. It is important to change this water daily in order to maintain the freshness of the curd.

### wasabi

Often referred to as Japanese horseradish because of the affect it has on the sinuses, wasabi is in fact a herb. Sold as a paste or powder, the paste needs to be mixed with a little water.

### wonton wrappers

These small, square-shaped pieces of dough made from flour and eggs can be found in refrigerators or freezers in Asian supermarkets.

# index

almonds: crunchy cabbage, egg, almond and noodle salad 43

barbecue pork with asian greens 90
beef: garlic, pepper and lemongrass beef with noodles 85
  spicy coconut beef and noodle salad 52
  vietnamese beef noodle soup 26
buckwheat noodles 10–11

cabbage: crunchy cabbage, egg, almond and noodle salad 43
caramelized pepper pork noodles 75
cashews: sweet chilli pumpkin and cashew noodles 86
chicken: chargrilled chicken breast topped with green curry noodles 82
  chicken and vegetable noodle broth 18
  sesame and lime chicken noodle salad 40
  stir-fried rice noodles with chicken and basil 66
  udon noodle nests with teriyaki chicken 72
chilli duck and pineapple noodle salad 57
coconut: spicy coconut beef and noodle salad 52
crispy noodles 6

dried noodles 6
duck: chilli duck and pineapple noodle salad 57
  duck noodle pancakes 36

egg noodles 12–13
eggs: crunchy cabbage, egg, almond and noodle salad 43
  duck noodle pancakes 36

fish: spiced turmeric fish with fresh herbs and noodles 65

garlic, pepper and lemongrass beef with noodles 85

ginger: kumera ginger soup with sesame soba noodles 28
green tea noodles 10, 11
  with tofu and soy butter 76

hokkien noodles 12

kumera ginger soup with sesame soba noodles 28

laksa: easy prawn laksa 22
lamb: creamy peanut noodles with lamb satay sticks 62
lemongrass: garlic, pepper and lemongrass beef with noodles 85
  pork, peanut and lemongrass noodle salad 44

mango: sticky port and mango noodle salad 47
mung bean noodles 14
mushrooms: egg noodles with oriental mushrooms 81
  vietnamese spring rolls 37

noodles: making 6
  origin 6
  types 10–15
nuts: crispy noodle and five spice nut mix 30

pad thai, quick 70
pancakes: duck noodle pancakes 36
peanuts: creamy peanut noodles with lamb satay sticks 62
  pork, peanut and lemongrass noodle salad 44
pineapple: chilli duck and pineapple noodle salad 57
pork: barbecue pork with asian greens 90
  caramelized pepper pork noodles 75
  pork, peanut and lemongrass noodle salad 44
  sticky pork and mango noodle salad 47

prawns: crispy prawn summer noodle salad 58
  easy prawn laksa 22
  prawn noodle toast 27
  prawn and scallop noodles 91
pumpkin: sweet chilli pumpkin and cashew noodles 86

rice noodles 14, 15
rice wine 80

salads 40–59
salmon noodle bonbons 33
sashimi noodle salad 56
scallops: prawn and scallop noodles 91
singapore street noodles 80
soba noodles 6, 10
somen noodles 11
soups 18–21, 26, 28
spinach: stacked soba and spinach salad 48
spring rolls, vietnamese 37
squid: warm lemon squid noodle salad 51
stir-fries 62–91

tofu: green tea noodles with tofu and soy butter 76
  quick pad thai 70
  tangy sweet-and-sour tofu and vegetables with noodles 71
  udon broth with agedashi tofu 21
tuna: sashimi noodle salad 56

udon: broth with agedashi tofu 21
  udon noodle nests with teriyaki chicken 72
  udon noodles 11

vegetables: chicken and vegetable noodle broth 18
  tangy sweet-and-sour tofu and vegetables with noodles 71
vietnamese beef noodle soup 26
vietnamese spring rolls 37

wheat noodles 10–11